Christmas Details

Christmas details

Mary Norden

photography by **Sandra Lane**

RYLAND
PETERS
& SMALL

LONDON NEW YORK

To the Garrads, for all the
wonderful Christmasses

Designer Sally Powell
Senior editor Annabel Morgan
Recipe editor Maddalena Bastianelli
Location research Kate Brunt
Production Meryl Silbert
Publishing director Alison Starling
Art director Gabriella Le Grazie
Stylist Mary Norden
Recipes Kathy Man

First published in the USA in 2000 by HarperCollins.
This paperback edition first published in 2006 by Ryland Peters & Small, Inc.
519 Broadway, 5th Floor, New York NY 10012
www.rylandpeters.com

10 9 8 7 6 5 4 3 2 1

Printed and bound in China.

Library of Congress Cataloging-in-Publication Data

Norden, Mary.
  Christmas details / Mary Norden ; photography by Sandra Lane.
    p. cm.
  ISBN-13: 978-1-84597-295-0
  ISBN-10: 1-84597-295-3
  1. Christmas decorations. 2. Handicraft. I. Title.

TT900.C4N67 2006
747'.93--dc22

                              2006008483

contents

introduction

*T*he key to a successful Christmas lies in the title to this book –
attention to detail is all-important. Within these pages you'll
find plenty of inspiration for decorating ideas, grouped in different
themes to help you plan a coordinated look, whether you want a
country-style Christmas or a contemporary one. There are new ideas for
traditional festive elements, such as candles and wreaths, and
even alternative Christmas trees for modern interiors. You'll
also find instructions for elegant handmade cards, ingenious
ways to wrap presents, recipes for homebaked goodies, and
pretty table settings. Most of the ideas are inexpensive; all
are extremely simple. These elegant and imaginative details
will help you celebrate the festive season in style and make
it truly special for you, your family, and your friends.
Merry Christmas!

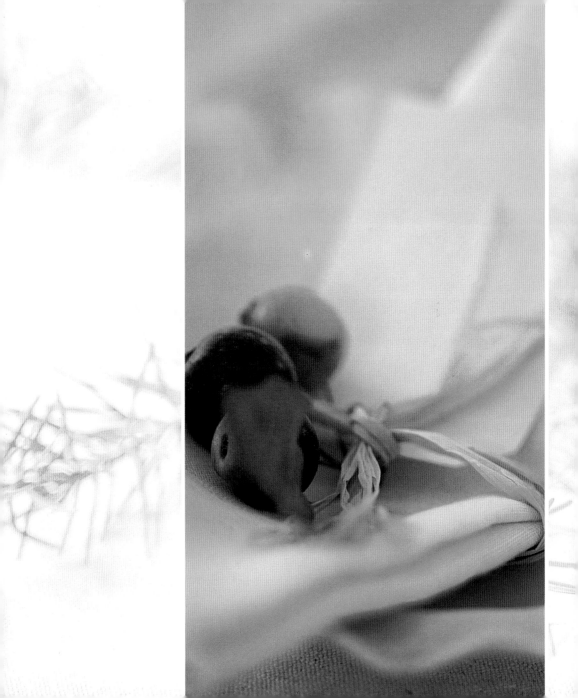

white christmas

For a white Christmas that doesn't rely on the weather, use pristine materials and simple decorative details to create a sophisticated scheme for house and table. Gather together white paper, bleached stones, creamy candles, and milky translucent glass. Look around notions departments for upholstery trims and unusual materials that will give your scheme an original edge. Remember, since you are not using color or pattern, texture will play a more important role.

This page and opposite: Pompom braid—sold by the yard to edge cushions and curtains— can be cut into short lengths and used to secure rolled napkins instead of a traditional ring. Alternatively, place a chalky white stone trimmed with thin silver cord atop a folded napkin. Repeat the theme by adding more pebbles along the length of the table.

setting the scene

There's something very decadent about feathers.
Use them to trim napkin rings, made from
equally glamorous sequin braid, and to fashion
a soft, fluffy, festive wreath.

Opposite: Roll up stiffly starched damask napkins and secure them with strips of sequin braid or other tactile trimmings. Tuck a feather into each one.

Right: Milk-glass tumblers stand on a length of intricate, handmade Japanese paper embossed with circles. Use unusual paper as a table runner or, alternatively, cut it into rectangles and use as table mats.

Left: A festive feather wreath is easy to make. Use a wire coat hanger and snip off the hook with pliers or, if you prefer, retain it to hang the wreath from. Buy a cheap feather boa and secure one end to the wreath base with a twist of fine wire or tape; then just wind the feathers around. Tuck in the end and leave the wreath plain, or add silver balls and bows. Hang on a door using a loop of white satin ribbon, or hook casually over a chair, as shown here.

Left: A snowy place setting is composed of all-white elements with a variety of different textures, from the smooth glass tumbler to the crisp damask napkin and the fragile Japanese paper.

white winter boughs

You don't have to go without a Christmas tree just because a traditional fir won't suit a simple white decorating scheme. Instead, reinvent the tree for a modern interior, using bold graphic lines and plain frosted balls.

Above: Rather than hanging lights from the branches, think of other ways to use them, such as winding them around the container that holds the willow boughs.
Right: Resist the urge to add gaudy colored balls. Cool frosted shapes enhance branches lightly dusted with white.

For a totally modern effect, complement a restrained white scheme with an understated "tree" made from branches of twisted willow. Contorted willow or hazel branches are available from florists. To give them a subtle dusting of white, spray them lightly with white spray paint. Stand the branches in a galvanized metal bucket and use crumpled newspaper, pebbles, or sand to hold them upright. For a strictly white theme, wrap presents in pristine white tissue paper and tie them with frosty white or silver ribbon.

Above: Intriguing decorations are made by cutting stars from silver or white posterboard and slipping them inside parchment-paper envelopes. Other shapes also work well.
Left: These tiny, fleecy white baby socks secured with café clips make enchanting and unusual tree decorations.

white

Above: Instead of candlesticks, use small white porcelain bowls. Anchor candles in the base and then surround with gravel.
Right: Use a glass vase filled with white gravel (available from garden centers) to hold tapers. For real drama, you can set them in a big galvanized metal bucket.

pure and simple candles

Candles may be centuries old, but they can be used in strikingly contemporary

ways. Mass a handful of tall, thin tapers together in a vase or bucket, group

chunky altar candles on mantelpieces or table centers, and fill the festive

home with the inimitable warm and welcoming glow of candlelight.

Left and below: A massed group of candles of varying heights and thicknesses creates a generous and dramatic effect. Place the candles before a reflective surface, such as a glass wall or window, to enhance their glow. This arrangement would work equally well on a mantelpiece with a mirror behind it, or arranged down the center of a dining table. Surrounding the candles with large chalky white pebbles adds textural interest.

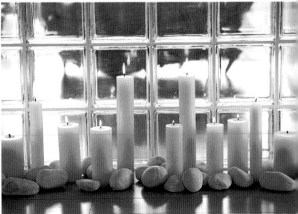

pretty packages

Wrapping small gifts stylishly (like wedding favors) means you can also use them as part of your table decorations. Make the gifts an integral part of each place setting—you could even label each one so they double up as name cards—or hand them around yourself after dinner.

The Christmas table offers an ideal opportunity to present tiny tokens with maximum impact. Even the simplest gifts can look glamorous with a little thought and preparation. Swathes of white tissue paper soon turn a chocolate into an exotic flower, while a ceramic dish can elevate a handful of candy into an elegant dinner-table adornment. Equally stylish presentation can be used when serving some of the food, too, from wrapping a warm bread roll in a napkin to stylishly packaging after-dinner mints or biscuits for coffee.

Right: Small white ceramic bowls filled with bonbons, with their characteristic dusting of powdered sugar, and finished with a white cord make thoughtful place settings and covetable small Christmas gifts, too.

Opposite: Fine chocolates laid on squares of pristine white tissue paper gathered with delicate organza ribbon can be handed out with dessert to be eaten at the table or even taken home as a party favor.

Opposite: A bread roll wrapped in a napkin and tied with white cord is ready and waiting for dinner to begin. **Right:** Serve after-dinner coffee with individually wrapped mints, packaged in white paper with a twist of ribbon. **Below**: Write guests' names on white labels, thread them on a length of white cord, and tie it around breadsticks for an unusual appetizer that doubles up as a place card.

*Presenting food stylishly pleases the eye
as well as whetting the appetite.*

traditional christmas

By using your imagination and thinking

more creatively, you can come up with

a reassuringly traditional Christmas scheme

that doesn't just fall back on good old holly

and mistletoe for decoration. Extend the

color palette beyond the traditional scarlet

by bringing opulent shades of maroon

and purplish-black into play. Instead of

plain green leaves, include hints of copper

foliage and the gleam of silver, and use these

rich, regal colors to decorate both table and

tree, incorporating seasonal fruits and

flowers wherever you can.

Opposite, above, and left:
Contrast the purple bloom
of ripe figs with the deep
velvety hue of red roses.
Pile the fruit on a platter;
then scatter rose heads
casually between pieces.
Cut the flower stems just
before you arrange them,
and they should last for
the rest of the day.

23

Right, far right, and opposite: Claret-red ribbon, coppery foliage, and a sprig of berries can be fashioned into a chic napkin ring. Try substituting a small bunch of red grapes or, for true luxury, rose heads for the berries.

decorating the table

Christmas dinner is one of the most important meals of the year and should be prepared for accordingly. Taking the time to plan and set a beautiful table shows guests how much you care, and contributes enormously to the sense of occasion.

If you have a fine oak or dark wood table, leave it uncovered so the rich, dark gleam of the wood is included in the overall look (you may want to use individual placemats to protect the table from hot dishes). Create a simple but effective centerpiece for the table using a glass cake plate piled high with an assortment of luscious fruits and extravagant red roses. Continue the strong and sumptuous color scheme by making your own napkin rings from lengths of crimson silk ribbon, a handful of fresh leaves, and a sprig of ruby-red translucent berries.

Right: A traditional-style Christmas tree can take plenty of decorations, but resist the urge to overdo things or you will conceal the shape and color of the tree itself. Here, three different sizes of balls in the same shade of rich scarlet have been supplemented with tiny white "crackers," lights and the occasional discreet sparkle of gold.

*When choosing a Christmas tree, look for one
that looks healthy and is a good shape. Shake
gently; if needles fall off, the tree won't last long.*

decorating the tree

**The popularity of the Christmas tree is due almost entirely to Prince
Albert, Queen Victoria's husband, whose enthusiasm for decorating
them caught on in the mid-1800s. Today we can choose from six or
seven different species, with needles in a variety of green shades.**

Above: Make miniature "crackers" to
decorate the Christmas tree. These
party favors contain a piece of candy
or a trinket. Roll up a piece of thin
card, place a small gift inside, and
tape in place. Cover the roll with a
piece of white crepe paper several
inches longer than the tube. Tie each
end with ribbon and a sprig of berries.
Lay the crackers on the tree branches.
Left: Rich red balls (suspended from
silky red twine) gleam in the warm
glow cast by tiny lights.

27

Right: Punctuate the basic wreath with clusters of brighter red fake berries. These come on soft wire stems and can easily be attached to the original wreath at intervals around the circumference. Add a plain red velvet streamer to match the new berries and hang the wreath over a door. If you don't want to damage the paintwork and there's a convenient coat hook on the other side of the door, hang the wreath on invisible fishing line and loop it right over the top of the door.

ringing the changes

A readymade wreath of artificial berries will last for years. A wreath can appear fresh and different each Christmas by dressing it with new accessories and using it in a variety of different ways—propped on a mantelpiece, as part of a candle arrangement or, in time-honored tradition, to decorate a door.

Left: Tie bows of red satin ribbon and slightly narrower plaid ribbon and wire them in pairs to your basic berry wreath for a pretty and colorful combination, ideal for the end of a mantelpiece or a sheltered front door.

Above: Weaving stems of fresh ivy through the wreath creates a more natural effect. On this hall shelf, three wreaths encircle groups of candles to create a dramatic welcome. Varying the height of the candles stops the effect from looking overly contrived. This arrangement would work just as well on a mantelpiece or a deep windowsill.

hanging decorations

Simple decorations are often the most charming.

Greenery hung from door handles and chair backs

brings Christmas cheer to every room in the house.

Hanging decorations can be made from whatever comes
to hand: a few trimmings from the Christmas tree,
a handful of berries—artificial or real—or spare balls,
preferably unbreakable. If you are using greenery for
door decorations, hang them on a generous loop of
ribbon so you don't get pricked every time you reach for
the handle. Don't forget fresh flowers, too. Red roses
are available all year round and team beautifully with
berries and evergreen leaves.

Above and right: Wind ivy on a thin wire ring, add a few red rose heads, and hang from a length of matching velvet ribbon.
Far right: Glue dried seedheads to a styrofoam ball and hang with ribbon for a robust decoration.
Opposite: Fir and berries are tied with red ribbon.

clever candleholders

Ordinary household items such as tea-glass holders or empty jars can be given a new lease on life as candleholders. With a little imagination, even the most mundane objects have new potential.

Look around the house and you will find some unusual and appealing candle holders, such as these old glass yogurt jars, which have a very pretty shape and need minimal decoration to transform them from discarded to desirable. If you are worried about the glass cracking as the candle burns down, pour a little water into the bottom of the jars. Whatever your candleholder, make sure the candle stands firmly upright (floral clay is useful) and keep an eye on them as they burn down, particularly when using foliage and berries to decorate them.

Right: A twist of ivy and a couple of beaded berries transform a simple glass jar into a pretty candle holder. It will also catch any dripping wax.

When used as candleholders, these old glass jars are transformed from discarded to desirable.

Above and opposite: The silver bases that hold Russian tea glasses also make perfect candle containers. Fill them with a handful of ivy leaves and berries and arrange a row of them along a mantelpiece or running the length of your dining table.

exotic christmas

To set the scene for an exotic Christmas, turn

to the riches of the East. The three Wise Men,

with their jeweled turbans and brocade robes,

carrying gifts of gold, frankincense, and

myrrh, inspire a color scheme of burgundy

and maroon shot through with metallic

thread, beaded decorations, and curtains of

stars. Heady perfumes and aromatics translate

into spicy pomanders and exotic sweetmeats.

This page and opposite: A circular mirror makes a beautiful and practical base for a candle arrangement, reflecting the glow of the flames and protecting the surface below from wax at the same time. Use tree candle clips to hold small candles around the edge of the mirror, place a large scented candle in the center and surround it with balls in precious metal colors.

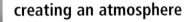

creating an atmosphere

Break away from the traditional Christmas colors of scarlet and green and imbue your home with the rich hues, warmth, and opulence of a more exotic time and place.

For an exotic Christmas, gather together the most sumptuous elements you can find—punched and engraved brass plates that gleam like dull gold, richly colored and decorated glassware, and rich velvet or tapestry floor cushions. The overall effect should be opulent, bold, and very exotic, using lots of burnished gold and jewellike colors.

Opposite and left: Exotic kumquats are served in a fluted amber glass bowl. **Far left:** A brass plate glints golden in the candlelight. It holds sweetmeats made from dried fruit, nuts, and spices—suitably exotic fare.

Opposite and below:
Display the pomanders on a suitable container—in this case an engraved metal Moroccan tray on legs.

spicy pomanders

The tang of oranges mingling with the spicy scent of cloves is an unmistakably festive smell. Homemade pomanders not only smell delicious, but can be decorative, too. They also make great gifts. Follow these tips to create your own designs.

When oranges are studded with cloves, they are transformed into pomanders, made the same way since medieval times. Orange peel can be tough, so prick your design first with a small skewer and then push the cloves into the holes. Tie the finished pomanders with a loop of ribbon and hang from window catches and door handles. Alternatively, arrange them along a mantelpiece, scattered among candles, where the warmth from the flames will intensify their scent.

Right: In addition to trimming gift bags, beads can add a sparkle to all kinds of unexpected objects. Here, an old-fashioned wire cake rack is turned into a festive tray by adding a fringe of jewel-colored glass beads. For each large bead, you will need a small bead to act as a "plug" and hold it in place. Thread a needle, tie the end of the thread to the cake rack, and pass it through the larger bead, then the smaller one. Loop the thread around the outside of the small bead, then back through the large bead. Loop thread around the wire rack and continue.

beads, baubles, and jewels

The possibilities for decorating with beads are unlimited. Stitch them to fabrics, thread them on fine wire, or simply display handfuls in glass bowls and jars—they look beautiful just as they are. Look for necklaces of real glass beads in thrift stores or flea markets, recycle broken necklaces, or buy beads from specialized suppliers.

Dainty gift bags make ideal packaging for small presents and look especially glamorous when trimmed with delicate, sparkling glass beads. To make a bag, cut out two pieces of silk, each 7 x 7in (18 x 18cm). Place the pieces of fabric right sides together, and stitch along the bottom and two sides, leaving the top open. Turn the bag right side out, make a small fold at the top, and hem. Cut a generous length of colorful cord, loosely gather up the neck of the bag, and wrap the cord around the bag several times before tying in a floppy bow. To decorate your bag, choose beads that complement the color of the silk. This bag was trimmed with beaded tassels; you can use your imagination to devise other designs.

Above left: Opulent gold-colored flatware is wrapped in a pristine linen napkin and tied with beaded cord.

Above center: An old-fashioned glass candy jar is ideal for displaying beaded baubles that look just as precious as finely crafted jewelery.

Above right: Scraps of exquisitely beaded braid or embroidered ribbon won't be wasted if you use them to embellish plain Christmas tree balls. Carefully remove the ball's metal neck and wire loop. Anchor the ribbon or braid around the circumference of the ball, using either strong glue or double-sided tape if the decoration is temporary. Replace the wire loop and neck to cover any untidy ends. To give decorated balls as gifts, leave one at each place setting, perhaps attached to a napkin.

Opposite: This collection of glass beads displayed in an old amber-tinted glass seem every bit as exotic and glittery as true gemstones.

A collection of richly colored glass beads displayed in an old amber-tinted glass seem every bit as exotic and glittery as true gemstones.

festive wreath

A readymade twig wreath is the base for a whole range of different

Christmas designs. Adorn it with greenery for the duration of the

holidays or make it into a long-lasting ornament, as shown here.

A readymade twig wreath is the basis for a festive wreath decorated with tiny presents and a scattering of stars.

To make this wreath, you will need a readymade twig wreath, gold spray paint, gold wrapping paper, gold ribbon, small bouillon cubes, and a length of gold wire studded with stars (or similar). Lay the wreath on newspaper and spray with gold paint (two or three light coats are better than one heavy coat). Let it dry while you wrap the cubes in gold paper to look like tiny presents. Tie each cube with ribbon. Use a hot glue gun or strong adhesive to attach the presents to the wreath at regular intervals. Finish by winding the starry gold wire around the wreath and tucking in the ends.

table decorations

In exotic shades of burgundy and bronze with hints of olive green, this sophisticated table shimmers in the candlelight. The rich colors and the simplicity of the decoration makes a welcome change from the ubiquitous Christmas colors of red and green.

Burgundy and bronze vintage sari fabric makes an unusual and eye-catching runner for this pared-down yet exotic Christmas table. The colors are picked up in the tarnished gilt balls lined up along the length of the table and in the small ones used to decorate the napkins. Chunky candles complete the look.

Above: Filled with small white candles that stand amid a sea of bronze balls, this white china cake plate forms a pretty centerpiece that casts a warm glow over the table.
Right and far right: Vintage silk sari fabric makes a richly colored runner.

This page: Tie rolled napkins loosely with ribbon and thread on a couple of small balls that coordinate with the rest of the table setting.

To make the stars you will need delicate gold paper, acetate film, and nylon fishing line. Before you cut out the stars, glue the paper to the acetate to reinforce it. Once cut out, the stars are then threaded on lengths of fishing line. Thread the line onto a needle and push the needle through the top and bottom of each star. Make a knot below each star to stop it from slipping down. Suspend the strings from nails or thumbtacks.

curtain of stars

Suspend a shower of gold stars across a doorway or window to create the most festive curtain imaginable, using the most inexpensive materials.

Opposite, left and above: Any kind of paper can be used for the stars, but this lacy gold paper creates a particularly ethereal effect.

49

sparkling votives

Humble votive candles are cheerful and cheap enough to mass together in generous quantities. They are invaluable at Christmas, when they can be scattered on tables, mantelpieces, and sideboards.

Instead of placing votive candles in glasses, why not jazz up their tin containers with a clever trick or two? Cut sparkly lace braid or another decorative trim into lengths that are slightly longer than the circumference of each candle, overlap the two ends, and anchor the braid neatly with glue or double-sided tape. As you won't be constrained by price, mass the candles by the dozen on flat mirrors, metal platters, and trays. As well as lace braid, you could also experiment with plush velvet ribbon, sequin trim, and beaded braid.

Above: Metallic braid with a delicate scalloped edge deceives the eye into thinking that these votive candles are held in filigree metal holders, an illusion further enhanced by placing them on a dull gold platter.

Right and opposite: Introduce a touch of silver to the table by tying napkins with thick silver cord. In keeping with this sleek, contemporary look, fasten with a chunky knot rather than a bow. **Below:** Lime-green balls and tree lights add sparkle to place settings.

contemporary christmas

Modern metallics set the tone for a completely contemporary Christmas. Mix shades of silver, pewter, and dazzling white with occasional flashes of strong, vivid color for a clean, modern look. Using unusual paper and ribbon is one of the easiest ways to bring metallic effects into the home.

modern metallics

A contemporary Christmas offers an opportunity to break away from tradition. Take inspiration from Asian-style dining and feast at a low-level table.

This setting continues the far-eastern theme, with simple gray silk tablemats placed diagonally, overhanging the table edges, and decoration pared down to just two elements—white tree lights and balls.

This page and opposite: Surprise guests with a string of tree lights at the table and a scattering of shiny balls to enhance pure white china and plain, understated glassware.

With a little imagination,
unusual papers can be used to
create unique table settings
that don't cost a fortune.

Paper is enormously useful when decorating a Christmas table. Specialized stationery and chain stores sell a vast selection of unusual papers, and with a little imagination they can be used to create unique table settings that don't cost a fortune. Crinkled paper with a leathery texture makes ideal table mats. Longer lengths could run across the table, linking one place setting to its opposite number. And a roll of wrapping paper would make an elegant runner, stretching from one end of the table to the other.

Above: A collection of frosted and engraved balls piled high in a fragile glass bowl makes a suitably silvery and shimmering centerpiece for a marvelously modern meal.

Opposite and left: Richly textured silver paper has been cut into squares to create unusual table mats. Instead of tree lights, a row of tiny votive candles runs the whole length of the table. Each guest has two napkins that have been starched, folded, and laid to form a neat cross. In addition to looking decorative, two napkins are a practical note for an extended Christmas dinner with several courses.

A placemat of folded metallic paper combined with dishes that are similar in feel creates a thoroughly modern table setting.

Above: Textured paper like the silver corrugated square shown here makes ideal table mats. Fold strips into matching napkin rings.

Opposite: Pleat thick paper into table mats (it should crease easily without the need for scoring). The bronze wallpaper shown here is a perfect match for the dull pewter tumbler and plate.

Left: To decorate napkins, keep your eyes open for off-beat tree decorations like this airy construction of wire and beads.

novel napkins

Instead of using conventional napkin rings, create

your own using a medley of different-sized,

shaped and colored ribbons and cords. Keep to

metallic shades and finishes to maintain the theme

but tie each napkin differently to add to the fun.

Opposite and left: Damask napkins are tied with a selection of braids, ribbons, and cords, all reflecting a shiny metallic theme.
Below: A roll of pleated metallic ribbon can be cut into lengths to wrap napkins with panache. Add a strip of sequin braid—choose square-cut or round sequins with an understated flat finish rather than the usual gloss.

To have an endless supply of different napkin rings at your fingertips, invest in a selection of braids, cords, and ribbons. Don't underestimate how much you'll need—allow a good 16 in (40cm) of cord or braid for each napkin. Wind your chosen cord generously around a rolled napkin—two or three times is best—and finish with a plain knot. To make a napkin ring of wide pleated ribbon, allow 8 in (20cm) of ribbon and wrap it around the rolled napkin; then add contrasting silver cord and tie in a smart knot to hold the ribbon securely in place. For a lavish, extra frilly effect, use twice as much ribbon and wrap it around in a double layer.

Opposite: Candleholders made from pleated metallic ribbon wrapped around a glass votive or jelly jar ideally complement silver table mats.

Left: Jars, vases, or other candleholders can be transformed by a surround of pleated metallic paper. You'll get best results with straight-sided containers.

contemporary candles

Candles add instant style to a table. Increase their impact with unusual containers and imaginative presentation for a contemporary Christmas table.

Pleated and corrugated paper and ribbon can also be used to transform plain glass jars or vases into elegant candleholders at minimal cost. Choose ribbon that is slightly deeper than the votive holder you want to cover. Cut a length of ribbon to the circumference of the holder, wrap the ribbon around, and glue or tape it in place. Use candles that are lower in height than their container, and NEVER leave them burning unattended. Paper can also be used to disguise jars or candlesticks. Cut a piece of paper the required height and twice the circumference of the container. Fold the paper every ³⁄₄in (2cm) to form pleats. Wrap it loosely around the container—if you pull too tight you'll destroy the pleats.

63

Vases, cans, jars, and glasses can all be pressed into service as candle holders. Once they have been covered with paper or ribbon, no one need know what is underneath.

Before you get busy with paper, scissors, and glue, first take a minute to consider the intended setting for your candles and holders. A row of short candles is much better suited to a long, narrow dinner table than one large candle in the center, while on a side table, a group of candles of varying height will add more interest than a single candle. However, a round dinner table works well with one large single candle or a cluster of candles placed in the center. Vases, cans, jelly jars, and drinking glasses can all be used as different-sized candle holders. Once they have been covered with a layer of pretty paper or a length of glittery ribbon, no one need know what is underneath.

Right: Wrap small glasses, jars, or votive holders with silver or gold crepe paper so that, when lit, the candle within casts a mellow glow. Make sure you cut a piece of paper that is slightly taller than the container and wider than its circumference. Fold over any raw edges and glue the overlap neatly in place.

Left: Use corrugated paper to disguise flower vases and turn them into contemporary candle holders. Fill tall vases with gravel to within 2in (5cm) of the rim; then place the candle on top and pack more gravel around the candle to hold it securely in place. If you've left it too late to buy gravel or stones, raid the pantry and use rice instead.

hanging lanterns

Paper lanterns make perfect Christmas decorations and are so easy to make. If you don't have a mantelpiece to dress festively, string a group of lanterns in a front window to welcome visitors.

Paper lanterns couldn't be simpler to make, but if you don't feel confident, start by practicing on some scrap paper. Fold a sheet of letter paper in half lengthwise. Every ½ in (1.5cm) or so, make a cut through the fold, stopping about ½ in (1.5cm) from the top edges. Unfold the paper and roll it into a cylinder, overlap the two edges and glue them together. Thread a darning needle with thin cord and stitch a loop to hang the lantern up with. You can create variations by using different weights of paper and different patterns. To add interest, vary the heights and sizes of the lanterns and glue scraps of sequin braid or ribbon around the tops and bottoms.

Opposite and left: These lanterns have been cut from a selection of silver and gold patterned paper and hung with glitter thread at a window. Some have been embellished further with strips of upholstery braid glued to the top and bottom rims.

Left: Tinsel bands contrast with silvery twigs.

Below: Beaded Christmas tree trim can be used in the same way for a sparkling, glittering effect.

Right: Christmas tree stars gain a new lease on life when set at intervals around the wreath.

silver wreath

Take one readymade twig wreath and dress it in three different ways to create a glittering contemporary decoration ideal for a front door or wall.

First, spray the twig wreath with silver paint. You will get a better finish if you apply several thin coats of paint rather than trying to cover the wreath in one heavy coat. When the paint has dried completely, decorate the wreath using one of three techniques: use a glue gun to attach Christmas tree stars at intervals around the wreath; wrap the wreath with a neat spiral of old-fashioned tinsel and glue the ends in place; or twist beaded Christmas tree braid around it in a similar fashion.

A readymade twig wreath provides a
versatile base for a glittering silvery wreath
that can be redecorated every year.

country christmas

Christmas in the country is a relaxed family affair, traditional yet simple, using materials gathered from the yard and the hedgerow to create an informal rustic setting for the festivities. Berries and greenery, antique linens and chunky candles all have their part to play in creating a simple red and creamy-white scheme.

Opposite: A bough of crab apples (above left) forms a simple centerpiece for this country Christmas table, with candles arranged at intervals along each side. Antique linen towels make perfect placemats, while napkin rings are formed from flexible birch twigs and a spray of snowberries (above right).

table settings and decorations

Berries and fruit of all kinds can be used to create festive table

settings. Choose from pearly snowberries, rosy crab apples, or scarlet

rowan berries—provided the birds haven't got there first! If bushes

are bare, very realistic-looking artificial berries are now available.

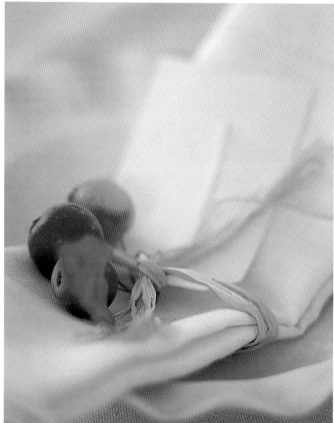

Far left: A folded napkin is tied with raffia and a cluster of crab apples.

Left: A mini galvanized-metal bucket is filled with berries and autumn leaves, but you could substitute ivy or a sprig of holly.

Opposite and below: Tie napkins with flexible twigs (thin birch twigs are ideal), then tuck in a sprig of evergreen foliage and snowberries. Arrange the napkins in a basket with pine cones and greenery.

Below: For a glowing ball of light, fill a galvanized-metal bucket or a similar container with sand; then firmly push in beeswax tapers. Place in a window or porch to greet visitors.

Right: The enamel basin belonging to this old washstand is the ideal home for a display of larger candles. Alternatively, you could buy a new enamel basin and place it on the floor or a side table.

Opposite below and detail: Many decorations are surprisingly versatile. Here, a berried wreath doubles as a candle holder.

country candles

Candlelight is mellow, intimate, and magical; and lighted candles bring an immediately festive atmosphere to any room. Stand candles on mantelpieces, mass them on windowsills, or position them in the center of the table. Remember that candles make more impact when they are used _en masse_, so be generous with quantities.

A foliage, berry, and fruit wreath makes a bold table centerpiece or a welcoming arrangement in a hall. Readymade wreath bases made from florists' foam are available in various sizes, as are circular plastic frames that hold the wreath and protect the surface beneath. Submerge the foam and frame in a bowl of water; when it stops bubbling, the foam is wet through and ready to use. Randomly push short lengths of foliage and sprays of berries into the wreath, letting them spill generously over the sides to conceal the plastic frame. To make a stem for the apples, firmly push a length of florists' wire through the base of the fruit. Bring the two ends of the wire together and twist tightly into a stem. Push the wire stems deep into the foam to hold the apple in position. Finally, place the candles in the center of the wreath and light them.

A row of candles on a windowsill greets visitors with a festive sight.

Opposite and below: An idea of utter simplicity and great charm. Thick glass jars double as votive holders, each one adorned with a twist of variegated ivy, whose glossy leaves catch the candlelight. Wrap the ivy tightly just below the rim of the jars and secure by twisting the ends together— use a piece of wire if necessary.

Opposite: The simplest arrangements suit an informal country setting. An armful of stems loosely massed in a well-worn bucket harmonizes well with scrubbed floorboards and modest furnishings. Mistletoe would make a good alternative, with its pretty foliage and near-translucent berries arranged in a cascade tumbling toward the floor. **Below:** Continue the foliage theme on a festive table by winding lengths of ivy around water glasses.

decorative foliage

Decorating the house with greenery at the bleakest time of year is a tradition that dates back to pagan times. Even today, we still appreciate the cheerful color and form of evergreens during winter when most other plants are dormant.

This Christmas, why not break away from traditional holly, mistletoe, and pine cones and look for alternative foliage and berries to deck the halls with? It's surprising what you can find, even in a small urban backyard— look out for shiny black viburnum berries, waxy snowberries or rosehips in different shapes and sizes— any plants with brightly colored berries and glossy, prettily shaped evergreen leaves are ideal. Whatever you collect from the great outdoors, keep your arrangements deliberately casual. Use rustic, country-style containers— galvanized-metal buckets, food jars, or plain enamel pitchers—rather than fine crystal or china vases.

Greenery and berries make stunningly simple Christmas decorations, and it's amazing how much you can find in your own yard.

Right: A cream-glazed earthenware milk pitcher makes the perfect foil for a bunch of freshly cut, heavily berried viburnum (*Viburnum tinus*). Other good plants for berries include pyracantha—which has the drawback of being rather spiky—and cotoneaster, which has fiery foliage as its leaves die. The candy boxes beneath this arrangement are tied with raffia and dried hops.

There are many possibilities for eye-catchingly different foliage decorations. Boughs of blue spruce or Sitka spruce, Fraser fir, or limber pine, can be informally arranged on mantelpieces or draped around pictures or mirrors. Glossy evergreen leaves also work well as Christmas foliage—try the dark-green, elegantly shaped leaves of mountain laurel. If you live in a warmer climate, magnolia leaves make an excellent alternative.

Left: A generous bunch of freeze-dried hops tied with a cheery gingham ribbon makes a stunningly simple front door decoration.

Below: An elegantly spare circlet of snowberry leaves is wound on a thin wire hoop and held in place with florist's wire.

cookies and candles

For a country Christmas, choose a simple theme for your tree. Star-shaped cookies and real candles are a modest combination that possesses great charm and is extremely effective.

Once the only way of lighting a tree, real candles are making a comeback, and special spring-clip candle holders are available for purchase. Always remember to keep candles well away from other tree decorations, and NEVER leave the room while they are burning. Edible tree decorations are another well-established tradition. Cookie cutters come in all shapes and sizes, so experiment with different themes—hearts, Christmas trees, or gingerbread men. If you are handy with an icing gun, try embellishing shapes with icing details. Old-fashioned royal icing, made from powdered sugar and egg white, which hardens to a shiny finish, is ideal. Place your tree in a large container and leave plenty of space for presents underneath.

Opposite and above:
Spicy star-shaped cookies suspended from loops of pretty gingham ribbon make inexpensive Christmas decorations with a decidedly countrified feel (see recipe on next page).

To make a hole to thread the ribbon through, pierce each cookie with a skewer, ½in (1cm) from the edge, before you put them in the oven. The evocative scent of cloves and ginger adds to the festive atmosphere.

Right: In addition to decorating the tree, spiced cookies—plain or iced—are a novel way of decorating a present. Thread a cookie onto a piece of string and tie it to a longer length of ribbon to tie the package.

SPICED STAR COOKIES

¾ **cup unsalted butter, softened**

¾ **cup sugar**

1 medium egg, lightly beaten

1¾ **cups all-purpose flour**

½ **teaspoon baking powder**

¼ **teaspoon baking soda**

½ **teaspoon ground ginger**

½ **teaspoon ground cloves**

½ **teaspoon apple-pie spice**

Makes about 25 cookies

1 Beat the butter and sugar together until pale and fluffy. Beat in the egg, a little at a time, until thoroughly mixed.

2 Sift the flour, baking powder, baking soda and spices into a bowl, then stir into the egg mixture. Bring together to form a soft dough, wrap in plastic wrap and chill for at least 1 hour.

3 Knead the dough lightly to soften, then roll out to ¼in (5mm) thick. Cut out stars using a 4in cookie cutter.

Gather the trimmings, re-roll, and cut out more stars. Put them ¾in (2cm) apart on lightly greased cookie trays. Using a skewer, make a small hole in each star about ½in (1cm) from the edge.

4 Bake in a preheated oven at 350˚F for 10–15 minutes. Remove from the oven and leave to cool on the cookie trays, then transfer to a wire cooling rack. When completely cool, thread ribbon through the holes and tie. Store in an airtight container.

cards & decorations

Far right: To make this cutout card, cut a long rectangle of thick paper and mark three equal sections. Score between the sections and fold. Lay the card on a cutting mat and, using a stencil, cut out the motif from the middle section. Glue a piece of gold paper behind the cutout then fold over one-third of the card and glue it to conceal the gold paper.

Above: Using thick artist's paper, cut out two rectangles 6 x 8in (15 x 21cm). Fold each piece in half and make two holes, 1¼in (3.5cm) from top and bottom, on each fold. Lay one card on top of the other and thread the holes with ribbon, tying it in a bow. Collect dried leaves, spray them with silver paint, and glue a leaf to every other side of the card.

Right: Cut a long rectangle, again from thick textured artist's paper, and fold it in half. Cut a series of five-pointed stars from metallic paper (leftover wrapping paper will do). Glue them in a line across the center of the card, then place a smaller star within each. Stationers sell packs of gummed silver and gold stars that are ideal for this purpose.

handmade cards

Handmade cards are so much more personal than purchased ones, and they

need not be too difficult or time-consuming to make. Using just a few simple

tools and techniques, scraps of rich fabrics, glittery braids, silky ribbons, and

pretty paper can be transformed into stylish cards—the imaginative and

unusual results are bound to become treasured keepsakes.

Right: Turn a shutter or door into a festive gallery. Cut a length of ribbon to fit shutter or door panel and secure with removable adhesive or thumbtacks. Use paper clips to attach cards. **Below:** If you like to re-read cards, arrange them in a toast rack. Change the order daily to vary the display.

Opposite: Use these basic tips to create a variety of handmade cards. Start by cutting out cards from thick watercolor paper to your chosen size. Cut decorative shapes, such as stars, holly sprigs, Christmas trees, or bells from pretty paper or colored felt (an ideal fabric because it doesn't fray). Glue the shape to the card and decorate further, if desired, by sticking on sequins or glitter. Or try gluing ribbon remnants to a card in the shape of a cross and filling in the gaps with gummed gold and silver stars.

Decorate handmade cards with Christmas shapes cut from colored felt—an ideal fabric because it doesn't fray.

Left and below: Find new and imaginative ways to display your Christmas cards. This greeting tree is made from tall branches of contorted willow that have been stood upright in a container—use crumpled newspaper, coarse sand, or pebbles to hold them in position. The Christmas cards are attached to the branches with cord or ribbon loops, which have been fastened to each card with a paper clip. For other unusual display ideas, see also the ribbon gallery on the previous page.

christmas stockings

Colorful handmade children's Christmas stockings can be used year after year and fast become favorite treasures, eagerly awaited when the decorations are unpacked every December.

Felt is the best fabric for Christmas stockings: it doesn't fray and comes in a rainbow of colors. Cut out a paper pattern for the stocking (it's best to be generous—it's easy to inadvertently make them too small). Then cut out two stocking shapes. Decorate the front of one shape, leaving the other piece plain. Place the two shapes together, decorated side up, and sew by machine or use a simple running stitch.

Left and right: When decorating each stocking, use your imagination. Buttons can become balloons while sequins double as Christmas tree balls. Cut squares of felt as presents and use the stitches that secure them to the stocking to represent ribbon.

alternative tree toppers

No Christmas tree is properly dressed until it has its tree topper in place. Choose a generously sized readymade sequined star like the one shown below or—even better—make your own dazzling decoration that will last for years to come.

Above: Cut four thin strips of cardboard, 10in (25cm) long and ½in (1.5cm) wide. Spread each strip with glue and cover both sides with metallic ribbon the same length and width. Let them dry, then glue strips of sequin braid to the top of each strip. When dry, arrange the strips to form an eight-pointed star and secure each one at the point where they cross with glue. Use florist wire to fasten the star to the tree.

Right: Customize purchased decorations to make striking tree toppers. Two holes have been pierced in the back of this sequined star, and a length of florist wire threaded through to hold the star on the tree.

Left: To make this picture-bow topper, you will need about 1½ yd (1.4m) of metallic ribbon with wired edges and a length of florist wire. Cut the ribbon into two lengths measuring 25in (65cm) and 30in (75cm). Fold the longer piece into a loop and overlap the two ends at the loop's center back. Fold the shorter piece in two and place it behind the first loop to form a cross shape. Wrap florist wire tightly around the center of the cross to form a large bow. Use the ends of the wire to fasten the bow to the tree. Trim the ends of the ribbon and arrange the bow.

tree decorations

It's a Christmas ritual; the moment when the box of decorations is brought down from the attic or the top of the closet. By adding both handmade and purchased decorations every year, you'll soon build up a collection of family heirlooms.

Above left: Miniature presents for the Christmas tree can be made by covering bouillon cubes with scraps of wrapping paper and snippets of ribbon. To create a variety of shapes, try wrapping matchboxes, too, or even making your own tiny boxes from cardboard.

Above right: This tiny flowerpot filled with miniature balls is easy to make and decidedly superior to the average glass ball. Give tiny terracotta pots (from craft stores) a coat of gold spray paint. Fill them with crumpled tissue paper and glue gold beads over the surface (using a glue gun makes life much easier). To hang them on the tree, glue a length of narrow ribbon to the base of the pot and again close to the rim and tie it in a loop.

Left: Remnants of brocade and embroidered fabrics can be turned into elegant bags to decorate the tree. Simply cut a rectangle of fabric and fold it right sides together. Stitch two sides, turn right side out, and hem the top opening. Fill bags with spicy potpourri or a couple of sugared almonds, or fake it with tissue-paper filling. Then tie the neck with a scrap of ribbon.

Christmas decorations are now big business, and it's no longer a seasonal trade—some Christmas stores stay open all year round. So there's every opportunity to build up a treasured collection of glittering balls and other trinkets. Once you've amassed many different tree decorations, you can play it two ways. Either mix and match balls, stuffed and embroidered shapes, beaded decorations, and ethnic ornaments for an eclectic, global look. Alternatively, choose a theme each year and use just part of your collection. A single color could be a starting point, or you might choose a particular shape or motif as the basis for a decorating theme.

Opposite: Modern decorations imported from India resemble old heirloom ornaments and bring an air of antiquity to the tree.
Left: Fragile glass balls may fade and become tarnished with age, but that's all part of their appeal. Store them in a box with cardboard dividers or in eggboxes to prolong their life.
Above: Elaborate metallic openwork globes can form the basis for a silver and gold decorating theme.

101

Glass balls, beading, and tinsel are only the starting point for a collection of Christmas decorations. More and more ornaments come onto the market every year, allowing you to add to your treasure chest of decorations. Look out for unusual wooden figures, paper ornaments, and other novel decorations at Christmas craft markets and fairs: a great many are made in Eastern Europe, though some come from exotic destinations such as South America and Asia Pacific.

Above: Intricately folded tissue-paper shapes are perennially popular. Traditional forms include bells, fruit, snowmen, and colored globes. They fold flat when not in use, and the soft wire catches that hold them open tend to need reinforcing with tape after a few years.

Right: Wooden decorations are ideal for families with small children since they are more robust than balls. Naive painted santas, clowns, and snowmen are particularly charming.

Opposite: This glittery festive elephant adorned with ruffles and fancy ribbons is an Indian stuffed-cloth tree decoration. Why not collect a whole menagerie of animals? Look for fish bristling with gold sequin scales, embroidered cats, and red plush camels.

Look for unusual wooden figures, paper ornaments, and other novel decorations at Christmas craft markets.

wrapping & gifts

giftwrap ideas

Imaginatively wrapped presents can be just as much a part of the

Christmas setting as the tree they are piled under. Adding ribbon is

one of the easiest and most stylish ways to dress up a present.

Left: Old-fashioned pillboxes make perfect containers for special presents such as earrings or cufflinks. There's no need to wrap the box – simply tie it with ribbon.

Opposite: French paper candy bags make pretty giftwrapping. Place the gift inside, roll the top down, and punch two holes through the rolled paper. Thread with ribbon and tie.

Above: To make a gift bag, use a "mold" such as a book. Wrap a length of good-quality paper around the book and tape the seam, then neatly fold and tape one end. Slip the book out and crease the narrow sides to form a bag shape. Place the gift inside, fold over the top edge twice, then wrap ribbon around the bag and tie.

Gift certificates or money are often welcomed

presents. Make them even more special by

disguising them in elegantly wrapped tubes.

While gift certificates or money are often welcome presents, they don't have to be presented in a plain white envelope. Instead, disguise gift certificates or bills in rolled tubes, which can be embellished in many ways. Cut squares of thin card stock, place the bills (in their envelope) on top, and roll up tightly. Tape in place, wrap, and tie with a ribbon.

Opposite: This selection of beaded hat pins came from an antique market. Tie them to the gift tubes with a length of gauzy ribbon (**above**) or use one to fasten a conventionally wrapped present, remembering to replace the safety cap on the pin.
Left: If you have several gift certificates to give, pile the decorated tubes in a pretty bowl, or add an extra ribbon loop and hang them from the tree.

Finish off a smartly wrapped present with a sparkling decoration or a sumptuous embroidered ribbon tied in a crisp bow.

Right: Gold is the theme for a trio of presents wrapped in shiny metallics.
Below: A stacked pile of presents are linked by a common color theme, but are wrapped in papers that have difficult textures.

Above: A sequined, star-shaped Christmas tree decoration adds a glittery finishing touch to a stylishly wrapped package, and gives someone two presents in one.

Above: Layering paper and ribbon is a particularly pretty way to wrap gifts. Wrap a broad strip of paper around the box or package, then place a narrower layer of paper or ribbon on top. Finish off with a sumptuous embroidered ribbon tied in a crisp bow.

111

candles

Candles make ideal gifts at this time of year when candlelight plays an important part in creating a festive atmosphere. Pretty wrappings can transform these inexpensive gifts into desirable luxuries.

Opulent wrapping paper and rich silk give candles added impact. By embellishing simple votive glasses and tying bundles of candles with an extravagant swathe of gauze or silk ribbon, you can create such a pretty effect that you shouldn't need to wrap them any further. Far better to let the candles themselves be part of the decoration. Be careful—keep tall, thin candles away from radiators or fires; they will warp in the heat.

Right: Personalize a candle in a plain glass votive by adding a band of ribbon, lightly anchored with glue, and a girdle of silky cord.

Opposite: A bundle of slim tapers bound in pleated silk and secured with a contrasting ribbon bow makes an irresistible gift.

Embellish votive glasses and bundles of candles with an extravagant swathe of silky ribbon to create a pretty effect.

Right: Rustic beeswax candles smell almost good enough to eat. Wrap them in an old-fashioned paper doily and tie with an elegantly ruffled ribbon for a welcome and useful gift.

Above and above left: Old teacups that have lost their matching saucers make pretty candle holders. You'll need some paraffin wax, available from craft stores in solid blocks or pellet form, and a length of wick. Melt the wax in a basin in a double boiler (never melt over direct heat).
Cut a length of wick and tie one end to a pencil. Rest the pencil on the cup so the wick is hanging in the center, and pour in the hot wax. When set, trim the wick.
Below left: Use the same technique to fill gold-painted flowerpots, first blocking drainage holes with florist clay.

115

Making your own sweetly scented gifts couldn't be simpler, as these lavender bags prove.

scented gifts

Scented presents are traditional Christmas gifts, whether they are a bar of luxury soap, a vial of precious perfume, or special products for the bath. And making your own sweetly scented gifts couldn't be simpler, as these potpourri sachets and lavender bags prove.

Opposite: No sewing required. Just place a handful of delicately scented potpourri or a bar of soap in the center of an antique handkerchief, scoop up the edges, and catch them with a ribbon in a coordinated color.

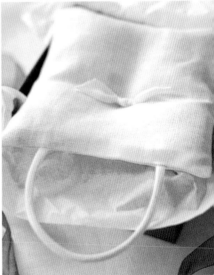

Above and left: Traditional lavender bags are given extra seasonal relevance when trimmed with a Christmas tree decoration. This pretty idea also works well for scented bath salts, but first put them in a plastic bag so they don't seep through the fabric.

edible treats

Gourmets are sure to appreciate a box or basket of the most indulgent homemade chocolate candy, made only from the finest ingredients.

The time and effort that go into homemade presents show friends and family how much you care. Chocolates are not complicated and are fun to make. One basic recipe (*see next page*) can be adapted to suit several different tastes—by rolling finished bonbons in chopped nuts, dusting them in cocoa powder, or decorating them with crystallized fruit, for example. Containers for homemade chocolates can include simple paper cones, small boxes lined with handmade paper, miniature bags, or even small wooden baskets.

Left and opposite:
Homemade gifts will always
be appreciated more than
bought ones because of the
thought, time, and effort
that they represent.

Indulgent, rich, and delicious, homemade chocolate truffles are the perfect gift—no less because they are so easy to make!

CHOCOLATE TRUFFLES

3 tablespoons raisins

1 tablespoon rum

2 tablespoons sugar

¼ cup hazelnuts, skins on

8 squares bittersweet chocolate

¼ cup unsalted butter

⅔ cup double cream

1 tablespoon brandy

For the coating:

½ cup unsweetened cocoa

⅓ cup chopped nuts, such as pistachios or almonds

4 squares bittersweet chocolate

1 square white chocolate

Makes about 27 truffles

1 Put the raisins in a small bowl, add the rum, cover, and leave to soak overnight.

2 Lightly grease a baking tray. Put the sugar and hazelnuts in a small, heavy-bottomed saucepan and heat gently until the sugar melts and starts to caramelize. Boil until golden brown, then pour onto the baking tray and let set. When hard, break the praline into pieces and crush to a coarse powder.

3 Melt the chocolate and butter in a heatproof bowl over a pan of simmering water, then stir in the cream. Let cool for 1 hour.

4 Divide the truffle mixture into three bowls: add the brandy to one, the rum-soaked raisins to the second, and the praline to the third. Let set in the refrigerator overnight.

5 For the rum and raisin truffles, sift the cocoa into a bowl, add teaspoonfuls of the truffle mixture, one at a time, and toss gently to coat in the cocoa.

6 For the brandy truffles, shape teaspoonfuls of the truffle mixture into balls, then roll in the chopped pistachios or almonds until completely covered.

7 For the praline truffles, melt the bittersweet chocolate. Using a fork, dip small balls of the truffle mixture into the chocolate to coat and shake off any excess. Put the truffle balls on parchment paper to set. Melt the white chocolate and drizzle over the truffles. Leave to set.

8 Store the truffles in the refrigerator for up to 1 week.

Above and right: Perfect presentation: these praline truffles have been casually drizzled with melted white chocolate, placed in tiny individual paper cases, and arranged on a dainty glass cake stand.

This page and opposite: If you don't have time to bake your own gifts, such as the cheese straws opposite, then buy some delicious cookies or crackers and repackage them more imaginatively, in pretty paper-lined boxes, for example, tied with ribbon.

CHEESE TWISTS

8oz frozen puff pastry, thawed
3 tablespoons wholegrain mustard
⅓ cup grated Monterey Jack
¼ cup freshly grated Parmesan

Makes about 36 twists

1 On a lightly floured surface, roll out the pastry to a rectangle, about 6½ x 16 in (16 x 40cm). With the short edge facing you, spread 1½ tablespoons of the mustard over the top two-thirds of the pastry, leaving a ½in (1cm) border. Sprinkle half of the cheeses on top of the mustard and press down gently.

2 Fold the uncovered bottom third of the pastry up over half the cheese, then carefully fold down the top third. Seal in the cheese by pressing the open sides firmly with a rolling pin.

3 Give the pastry a quarter turn. Repeat the rolling and folding process using the remaining mustard and cheeses.

4 Roll out the pastry to a rectangle, about 10¼ x 13½in (26 x 34cm). Trim the edges. Cut into strips, about ½ x 7in (1.5 x 17cm) and twist into spirals. Put 1in (2cm) apart on greased baking trays and bake in a preheated oven at 400°F for 15–20 minutes until puffed and golden.

5 Remove from the oven and let cool on the baking trays for 5 minutes, then transfer to a wire rack to cool completely. Store in an airtight container or freeze for up to 1 month.

SPICED NUTS

¾ cup each of blanched almonds,
hazelnuts, and cashews
1 tablespoon olive oil
½ teaspoon garlic salt
2 teaspoons jerk seasoning (available
from larger supermarkets, Caribbean
grocers or some delicatessens)

1 Put the nuts in a large bowl, add the olive oil and mix. Sprinkle the salt and jerk seasoning over and mix thoroughly.

2 Spread the nuts on a baking tray and bake in a preheated oven at 350°F for 12–15 minutes until browned. Leave until cool then store in an airtight container.

Makes about 2¼ cups of spiced nuts

If you are holding a party, leave a gift at each place setting. Alternatively, arrange small packages under the tree or hand to guests as they depart.

Homemade delicacies packed in imaginative containers look far more stylish than purchased foods. Unusual fabrics make pretty covers for jar lids, and cellophane bags are ideal for nuts and other oily foods or buttery cookies and truffles. If you plan to package cookies or chocolates in handmade paper or cardboard boxes, line them with parchment or waxed paper to stop oil from seeping through. There's no right or wrong way to give presents. If you are holding a party, leave a gift at each place setting. Alternatively, arrange small packages beneath the tree or hand them to guests as they depart.

Above left: A wooden basket like the ones strawberries are sometimes sold in is lined with Japanese paper and used to hold homemade cookies. A gingham ribbon completes the look.
Left: Repackage olives from the deli counter in a glass jar and top off with olive oil. The cap is made from a square of parchment paper topped with a scrap of open-weave fabric and held in place by a festive gold cord.
Opposite: Spiced nuts bagged in cellophane make perfect going-home gifts after a Christmas party.

sources

CHRISTMAS DECORATIONS

Bronners Christmas Wonderland
25 Christmas Lane
Frankenmuth, MI 48734
989-652-9931
800-ALL-YEAR (255-9327)
www.bronners.com
Literally thousands of lights, ornaments, nativities, and Christmas trees, plus more than 50,000 gifts and trims from around the world.

D. Blumchen & Co.
162 East Ridgewood Avenue
Ridgewood, NJ 07451
201-652-5595
1-866-OLD-XMAS
(653-9627)
www.blumchen.com
High-end Christmas decorations and items for other holidays, including Easter and Halloween.

Harrow Stores, Inc.
610 Route 110
Melville, NY 11747
631-752-2800

Harrow's Christmas season runs from September through January. They carry a large selection of lifelike trees, ornaments, lights, and collectibles.

Incredible Christmas Store
Trump Tower
725 Fifth Avenue
New York, NY 10022
212-754-1200
888-884-XMAS (9627)
www.incrediblechristmas.com
Christmas products from all around the world, as well as a selection of New York exclusive souvenirs.

RIBBONS AND TRIMMINGS

Elliot, Greene & Company
37 West 37th Street
New York, NY 10018
212-391-9075
212-391-9079 (fax)
Minimum order $25. They carry rhinestones, sequins, and beads of all description including some in glass, wood, plastic, and metal.

Hyman Hendler & Sons
67 West 38th Street
New York, NY 10018
212-840-8393
212-704-4237 (fax)
www.hymanhendler.com
Minimum order $50. Basic, novelty, and vintage ribbons.

M & J Trimming
1008 Sixth Avenue
New York, NY 10018
212-204-9595
1-800-9-MJTRIM
www.mjtrim.com
A wide range of trimmings and notions, including a good selection of buttons.

Ornamental Resources
1427 Miner Street
P.O. Box 3303
Idaho Springs, CO 80452
800-876-6762
www.ornabead.com
Minimum order $25. Carries rare, old, or unusual beads, including semi-precious stone beads, seed beads, druk beads, rhinestones, tassels, findings, and tools.

The Ribbonerie
191 Potrero Avenue
San Francisco, CA 94103
415-626-6184
www.theribbonerie.com
A range of both domestic and imported ribbons.

Tinsel Trading Co.
47 West 38th Street
New York, NY 10018
212-730-1030
www.tinseltrading.com
An extensive selection of vintage buttons, ribbons, flowers, and metallic trims.

Toho Shoji
990 Sixth Avenue
New York, NY 10018
212-868-7465
www.tohoshojiny.com
A range of embellishments, including beads, feathers, and jingle bells.

YLI Corporation
161 West Main Street
Rock Hill, SC 29730
803-985-3100
ylicorp@ylicorp.com (email)

www.ylicorp.com
Silk ribbons, hand-dyed ribbons, and decorative sewing threads.

PAPER AND CARDS

Blick Art Materials
1–5 Bond Street
New York, NY 10012
212-533-2444
888-828-4548
www.artstore.com
Specialty papers, art supplies, and studio furniture.

Jam Paper
135 3rd Avenue
New York, NY 10003
212-473-6666
800-8010-JAM
info@jampaper.com (email)
www.jampaper.com
Specializes in colored envelopes.

Jo-Ann
13323 Riverside Drive
Sherman Oaks
CA 91423-2508
(818) 789-3167
1-800-525-4951 for enquiries.
www.joann.com
Craft suppliers for all projects, branches nationwide.

Kate's Paperie
561 Broadway
New York, NY 10012
212-941-9816
888-809-9880
www.katespaperie.com
Over 40,000 exotic papers from around the world as well as elegant gifts, unique

stationery, journals, photo albums, and fine pens. Also offers paper-related services including custom printing, custom gift-wrapping, and corporate gifts programs.

Michaels
Call 1-800-MICHAELS for a store near you.
www.michaels.com
Specialty retailer of arts and crafts items, including rubber-stamping and découpage.

New York Central Art Supply
62 Third Avenue
New York, NY 10003
212-473-7705
800-950-6111
www.nycentralart.com
Minimum order $15. Specializes in unique and rare items and provides services for artists, such as priming canvas, stretching, and framing. Carries over 4000 handmade, moldmade, and machine-made sheets from around the world.

Papivore/Marie-Papier
117 Perry Street
New York, NY 10014

212-627-6055
info@papivore.com (email)
www.papivore.com
A large selection of Marie-Papier papers as well as other stationery items including journals, albums, note pads, and scrap books.

Sax Arts & Crafts
2725 S. Moorland Road
New Berlin, WI 53151
800-558-6696
www.saxarts.com
Art materials and a wide range of specialty papers.

The Written Word
1365 Connecticut Avenue
NW Washington DC 20036
202-223-1400
www.writtenword.invitations.com
Specializes in handmade papers and letterpress printing.

CANDLES

The Candle Shop
118 Christopher Street
New York, NY 10014
212-989-0148
800-223-7201
www.candlexpress.com

A wide range of candles and candle accessories.

Candleshtick
181 Seventh Avenue
New York, NY 10011
212-924-5444
A wide range of candles and candle-making supplies.

Covington Candle
976 Lexington Avenue
New York, NY 10021
212-472-1131
212-717-8186 (fax)
covcandle@aol.com (email)
Custom-made dinner and pillar candles in various colors and sizes, particularly more unusual sizes.

Illuminations
Mailing address:
1736 Corporate Circle
Petaluma, CA 94954
(707) 769-2700
1-800-621-2998
www.illuminations.com
Candles, candle accessories, and home-decor products.

Williamsburg Soap and Candle Company
7521 Richmond Road
Williamsburg, VA 23188
757-564-3354
www.candlefactory.com
Candles (mostly unscented) in many colors and sizes.

Yankee Candle Company
P.O. Box 110
South Deerfield
Mass 01373
800-243-1776
www.yankeecandle.com
Scented candles.

acknowledgments

First, I would like to say a big thank you to everyone at Ryland Peters & Small who has worked so hard to produce *Christmas Details*: Alison Starling, Gabriella Le Grazie, Megan Smith, Sally Powell and Kate Brunt. A special thank-you goes to my editor, Annabel Morgan, for her constant enthusiasm and support throughout the deluge of balls and tinsel. Also thanks to Kathy Man for all the festive cooking. Many, many thanks to my wonderful assistant, Kirsten Robinson, not just for her efficiency but also for her cheerfulness and keenness throughout. Thank you to Sandra Lane for her beautiful pictures and to her assistant Claudia Dulak. I would also like to thank my agent, Fiona Lindsay. As always, my husband has been constantly supportive, and wisely took work in Rio during the many weeks of Christmas upheaval here at home. A huge thank you.

The photographs on pages 2 and 44–48 are by Debi Treloar.

The author and publisher would like to thank Stephan Schulte and Sheila Scholes for allowing them to photograph in their homes.